Algebra Rules!

BRITANNICA
Mathematics in Context

Algebra

HOLT, RINEHART AND WINSTON

Mathematics in Context is a comprehensive curriculum for the middle grades. It was developed in 1991 through 1997 in collaboration with the Wisconsin Center for Education Research, School of Education, University of Wisconsin-Madison and the Freudenthal Institute at the University of Utrecht, The Netherlands, with the support of the National Science Foundation Grant No. 9054928.

This unit is a new unit prepared as a part of the revision of the curriculum carried out in 2003 through 2005, with the support of the National Science Foundation Grant No. ESI 0137414.

National Science Foundation
Opinions expressed are those of the authors
and not necessarily those of the Foundation.

Kindt, M.; Dekker, T.; and Burrill, G. (2006). *Algebra rules.* In Wisconsin Center for Education Research & Freudenthal Institute (Eds.), *Mathematics in context.* Chicago: Encyclopædia Britannica, Inc.

ISBN 0-03-038574-1

4 5 6   073   09 08 07

The *Mathematics in Context* Development Team

Development 2003–2005

The revised version of *Algebra Rules* was developed by Martin Kindt and Truus Dekker.
It was adapted for use in American schools by Gail Burrill.

Wisconsin Center for Education

Research Staff

Thomas A. Romberg
Director

David C. Webb
Coordinator

Gail Burrill
Editorial Coordinator

Margaret A. Pligge
Editorial Coordinator

Project Staff

Sarah Ailts
Beth R. Cole
Erin Hazlett
Teri Hedges
Karen Hoiberg
Carrie Johnson
Jean Krusi
Elaine McGrath

Margaret R. Meyer
Anne Park
Bryna Rappaport
Kathleen A. Steele
Ana C. Stephens
Candace Ulmer
Jill Vettrus

Freudenthal Institute Staff

Jan de Lange
Director

Truus Dekker
Coordinator

Mieke Abels
Content Coordinator

Monica Wijers
Content Coordinator

Arthur Bakker
Peter Boon
Els Feijs
Dédé de Haan
Martin Kindt

Nathalie Kuijpers
Huub Nilwik
Sonia Palha
Nanda Querelle
Martin van Reeuwijk

Cover photo credits: (all) © Corbis

Illustrations
3, 8 James Alexander; **7** Rich Stergulz; **42** James Alexander

Photographs
12 Library of Congress, Washington, D.C.; **13** Victoria Smith/HRW; **15** (left to right) HRW Photo; © Corbis; **25** © Corbis; **26** Comstock Images/Alamy; **33** Victoria Smith/HRW; **36** © PhotoDisc/Getty Images; **51** © Bettmann/Corbis; **58** Brand X Pictures

◆ Contents

Letter to the Student   vi

Section Ⓐ   **Operating with Sequences**

Number Strips and Expressions	1
Arithmetic Sequence	2
Adding and Subtracting Expressions	3
Expressions and the Number Line	6
Multiplying an Expression by a Number	8
Summary	10
Check Your Work	11

Section Ⓑ   **Graphs**

Rules and Formulas	13
Linear Relationships	16
The Slope of a Line	18
Intercepts on the Axes	20
Summary	22
Check Your Work	23

Section Ⓒ   **Operations with Graphs**

Numbers of Students	25
Adding Graphs	26
Operating with Graphs and Expressions	29
Summary	30
Check Your Work	31

Section Ⓓ   **Equations to Solve**

Finding the Unknown	33
Two Arithmetic Sequences	34
Solving Equations	37
Intersecting Graphs	38
Summary	40
Check Your Work	41

Section Ⓔ   **Operating with Lengths and Areas**

Crown Town	42
Perimeters	43
Cross Figures	44
Formulas for Perimeters and Areas	46
Equivalent Expressions	47
The Distribution Rule	48
Remarkable or Not?	49
Summary	52
Check Your Work	53

Additional Practice	55
Answers to Check Your Work	60

Dear Student,

Did you know that algebra is a kind of language to help us talk about ideas and relationships in mathematics? Rather than saying "the girl with blonde hair who is in the eighth grade and is 5'4" tall and…," we use her name, and everyone knows who she is. In this unit, you will learn to use names or rules for number sequences and for equations of lines, such as $y = 3x$, so that everyone will know what you are talking about. And, just as people sometimes have similar characteristics, so do equations ($y = 3x$ and $y = 3x + 4$), and you will learn how such expressions and equations are related by investigating both their symbolic and graphical representations.

You will also explore what happens when you add and subtract graphs and how to connect the results to the rules that generate the graphs.

In other MiC units, you learned how to solve linear equations. In this unit, you will revisit some of these strategies and study which ones make the most sense for different situations.

And finally, you will discover some very interesting expressions that look different in symbols but whose geometric representations will help you see how the expressions are related. By the end of the unit, you will able to make "sense of symbols," which is what algebra is all about.

We hope you enjoy learning to talk in "algebra."

Sincerely,

The Mathematics in Context Development Team

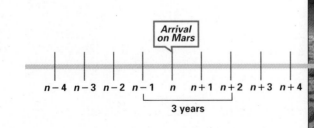

Operating with Sequences

Number Strips and Expressions

Four sequences of patterns start as shown below.

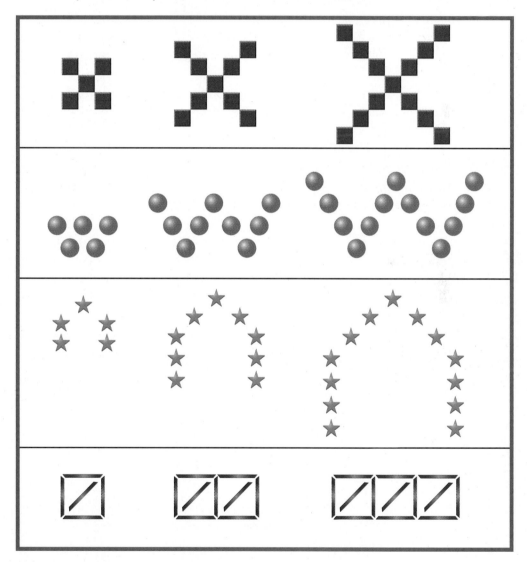

The four patterns are different.

1. What do the four patterns have in common?

You may continue the sequence of each pattern as far as you want.

2. How many squares, dots, stars, or bars will the 100th figure of each sequence have?

Arithmetic Sequence

The common properties of the four sequences of patterns on the previous page are:

- the first figure has 5 elements (squares, dots, stars, or bars);
- with each step in the row of figures, the number of elements grows by 4.

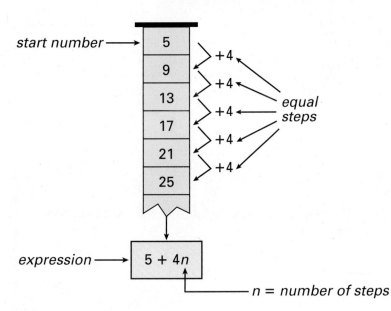

start number →

| 5 |
| 9 |
| 13 |
| 17 |
| 21 |
| 25 |

+4
+4
+4
+4
+4

equal steps

expression → 5 + 4n

n = number of steps

So the four sequences of patterns correspond to the same *number sequence*.

Remark: To reach the 50th number in the strip, you need 49 steps.

So take *n* = 49 and you find the 50th number: 5 + 4 × 49 = 201.

3. a. Fill in the missing numbers.

b. The steps are equal. Fill in the missing numbers and expressions.

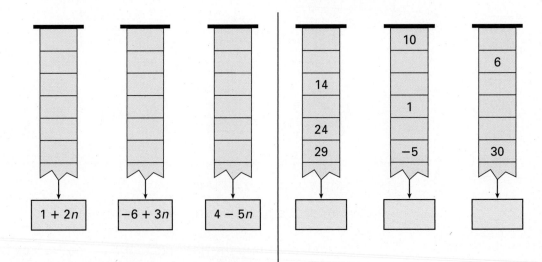

| 1 + 2n | | −6 + 3n | | 4 − 5n |

	14	24	29
10	1	−5
6	30

A number sequence with the property that all steps from one number to the next are the same is called an **arithmetic sequence**.

Any element *n* of an arithmetic sequence can be described by an expression of the form:

start number + step × n

Note that the step can also be a negative number if the sequence is decreasing.

For example, to reach the 100th number in the strip, you need 99 steps, so this number will be: $5 + 4 \times 99 = 401$.

Such an arithmetic sequence fits an expression of the form: start number + step × *n.*

Adding and Subtracting Expressions

Remember how to add number strips or sequences by adding the corresponding numbers.

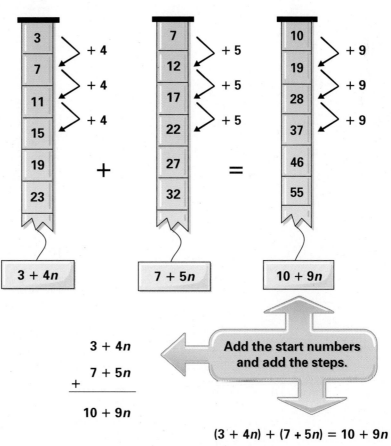

$$3 + 4n$$
$$7 + 5n$$
$$+ \overline{}$$
$$10 + 9n$$

Add the start numbers and add the steps.

$$(3 + 4n) + (7 + 5n) = 10 + 9n$$

4. a. Write an expression for the sum of $12 + 10n$ and $8 - 3n$.

b. Do the same for $-5 + 11n$ and $11 - 9n$.

5. Find the missing numbers and expressions.

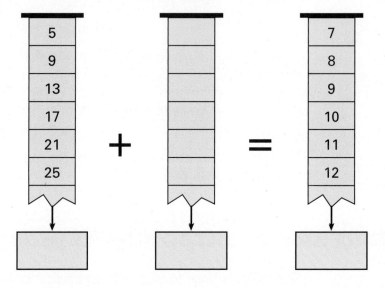

6. Find the missing expressions in the tree.

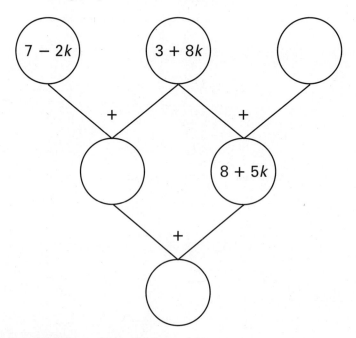

7. Find the missing expressions.

a. $(7 - 5n) + (13 - 5n) = \ldots\ldots$

b. $(7 - 5m) + \ldots\ldots = 12 + 5m$

c. $\ldots\ldots + (13 - 5k) = 3 - 2k$

8. a. Rewrite the following expression as short as possible.

$$(2 + n) + (1 + n) + n + (-1 + n) + (-2 + n)$$

b. Do the same with:

$$(1 + 2m) + (1 + m) + 1 + (1 - m) + (1 - 2m)$$

9. Consider *subtraction* of number strips. Fill in the missing numbers and expressions.

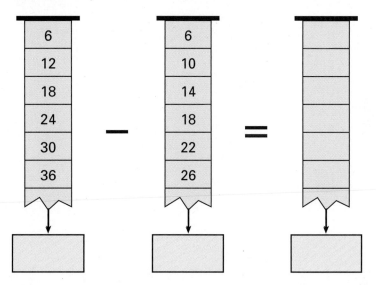

10. Find the missing expressions.

a. $(6 + 4n) - (8 + 3n) = $ ....

b. $(4 + 6n) - (3 + 8n) = $ ....

11. a. Fill in the missing numbers and expressions.

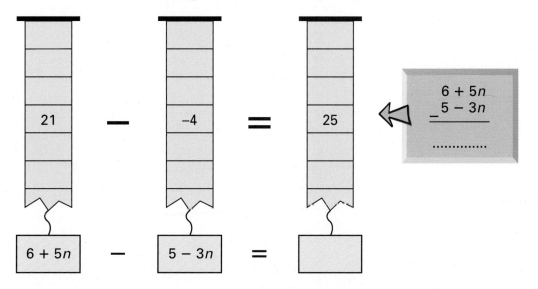

b. Do the same with:

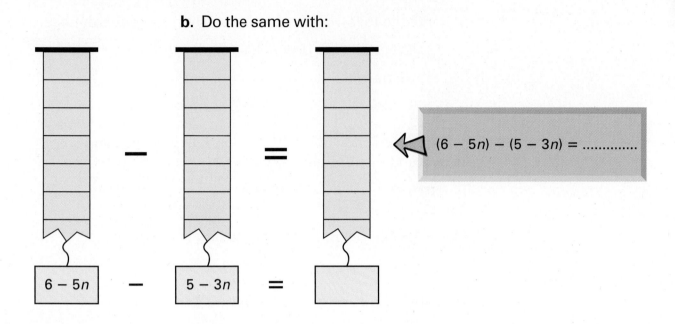

$(6 - 5n) - (5 - 3n) = \ldots\ldots\ldots$

| $6 - 5n$ | — | $5 - 3n$ | = | |

12. Reflect Write an explanation for a classmate, describing how arithmetic sequences can be subtracted.

Expressions and the Number Line

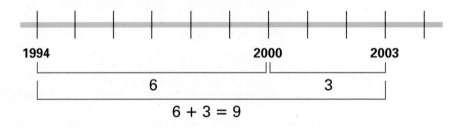

Between 1994 and 2003, there are 9 years.

13. How many years are there between 1945 and 2011?

In the year n, astronauts from Earth land on Mars for the first time.
One year later, they return to Earth. That will be year $n + 1$.
Again one year later, the astronauts take an exhibition about their trip around the world. That will be the year $n + 2$.

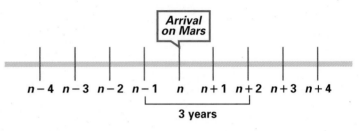

The construction of the launching rocket began one year before the landing on Mars, so this was in the year $n - 1$.

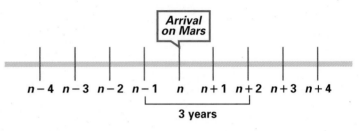

Between $n - 1$, and $n + 2$ there are 3 years. You may write:

$$(n + 2) - (n - 1) = 3$$

14. How many years are there between $n - 4$ and $n + 10$?

15. Calculate:

    a. $(n + 8) - (n - 2) = $ ....   **c.** $(n - 1) - (n - 4) = $ ....

    b. $(n + 7) - (n - 3) = $ ....   **d.** $(n + 3) - (n - 3) = $ ....

16. How many years are there between $n - k$ and $n + k$?

Even and **odd** year.

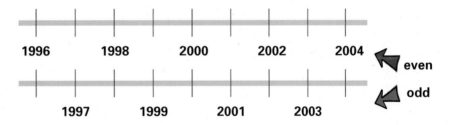

An even number is *divisible by 2* or is a *multiple of 2*. Therefore, an arbitrary *even* year can be represented by $2n$. In two years, it will be the year $2n + 2$, which is the even year that follows the even year $2n$. The even year that comes before $2n$ is the year $2n - 2$.

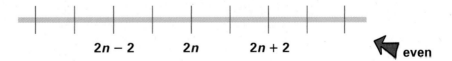

17. a. What is the even year that follows the year $2n + 2$?

    b. What is the even year that comes before the year $2n - 2$?

The *odd* years are between the even years.

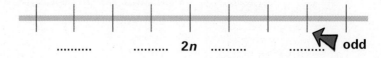

.... **2n** ....▼ **odd**

18. Write expressions for the odd years on the number line.

19. Find the missing expressions.

    a. $(2n + 8) - (2n - 6) = $ ....

    b. $(2n + 3) - (2n - 3) = $ ....

    c. $(2n + 4) - (2n - 3) = $ ....

Multiplying an Expression by a Number

Multiplying a strip or sequence by a number means: multiplying all the numbers of the sequence by that number. Example:

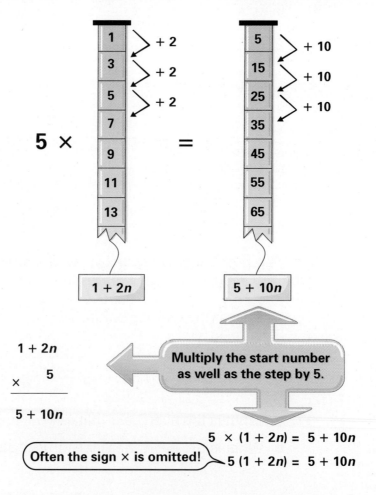

20. Find the missing numbers and expressions.

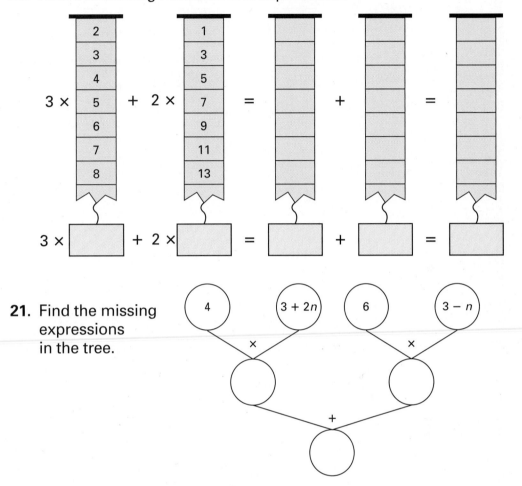

21. Find the missing
expressions
in the tree.

22. Find the missing expression. Use number strips if you want.

a. 5 (−4 + 3*n*) = ...

b. 3 (1 − 4*n*) = ...

c. 5 (−4 + 3*n*) + 3 (1 − 4*n*) = ... + ... = ...

23. Which of the expressions is equivalent to 4(3 − 5*m*)? Explain your
reasoning.

a. 12 − 5*m*   **c.** 7 − 9*m*

b. 12 − 20*m*   **d.** 4 × 3 − 4 × 5 × 4 × *m*

24. a. Make a number strip that could be represented by the
expression 4(3 + 8*n*).

b. Do the same for 5(−3 + 6*n*).

c. Write an expression (as simple as possible) that is equivalent to
4(3 + 8n) − 5(−3 + 6n).

Summary

The numbers on a number strip form an **arithmetic sequence** if they increase or decrease with **equal steps**.

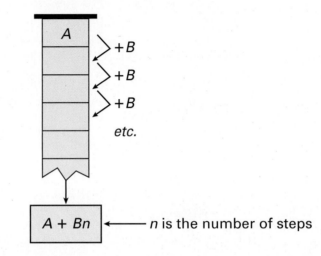

Adding two arithmetic sequences is done by adding the corresponding numbers of both sequences. You add the expressions by adding the start numbers and adding the steps.

Similar rules work for subtracting arithmetic sequences and their expressions. For example, written vertically:

$$+\quad\begin{array}{r} 20 + 8n \\ 7 + 10n \\ \hline 27 + 18n \end{array} \qquad -\quad \begin{array}{r} 20 + 8n \\ 7 + 10n \\ \hline 13 - 2n \end{array}$$

or written horizontally and using parentheses:

$$(20 + 8n) + (7 + 10n) = 27 + 18n$$

$$(20 + 8n) - (7 + 10n) = 13 - 2n$$

Multiplying an arithmetic sequence by a number is done by multiplying all the terms in the sequence by that number.

To multiply the expression by 10, for instance, you multiply the start number as well as the step by 10.

Examples:

$$10 \times (7 + 8n) = 70 + 80n$$

$$10 \times (7 - 8n) = 70 - 80n$$

or omitting the multiplication signs:

$$10 (7 + 8n) = 70 + 80n$$

$$10 (7 - 8n) = 70 - 80n$$

Check Your Work

1. Fill in the missing numbers and expressions.

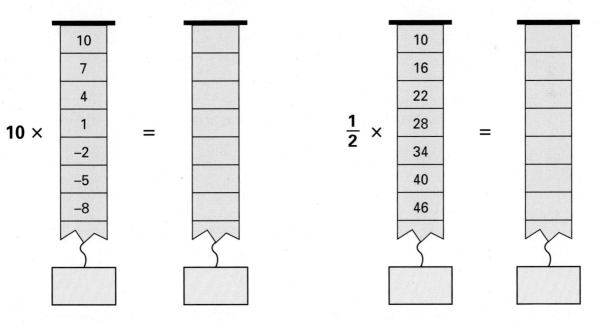

2. a. When will an arithmetic sequence decrease?

   b. What will the sequence look like if the growth step is 0?

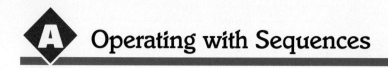
3. Give the missing expressions.

a. $12 - 18n$

$+\ \dfrac{18 + 12n}{\underline{\hspace{2cm}}}$

....

b. $22 - 11n$

$-\ \dfrac{19 - 11n}{\underline{\hspace{1.5cm}}}$

....

c. $26 - 25n$

$\times\ \dfrac{4}{\underline{\hspace{1.5cm}}}$

....

The election of the president of the United States is held every four years. George Washington, the first president of the United States, was chosen in 1788.

Below you see a strip of the presidential election years.

1788 | 1792 | 1796 | 1800 | 1804 | 1808 | 1812 | 1816 | 1820 | 1824 | 1828

4. **a.** Write an expression that corresponds to this number strip.

   b. How can you use this expression to see whether 1960 was a presidential election year?

5. Give an expression, as simple as possible, that is equivalent to $2(6 - 3n) + (5 - 4n)$

For Further Reflection

You have used number strips, trees, and a number line to add and subtract expressions. Tell which you prefer and explain why.

B Graphs

Rules and Formulas

Susan wants to grow a pony tail. Many girls in her class already have one.

The hairdresser tells her that on average human hair will grow about 1.5 centimeters (cm) per month.

1. Estimate how long it will take Susan to grow a pony tail. Write down your assumptions.

Assuming that the length of Susan's hair is now 15 cm, you can use this formula to describe how Susan's hair will grow.

$$L = 15 + 1.5T$$

2. What does the L in the formula stand for? And the T?

3. a. Use **Student Activity Sheet 1** to complete the table that fits the formula $L = 15 + 1.5T$.

T (in months)	0	1	2	3	4	5	...	
L (in cm)								30

b. Use **Student Activity Sheet 1** and the table you made to draw the graph that fits the formula $L = 15 + 1.5T$.

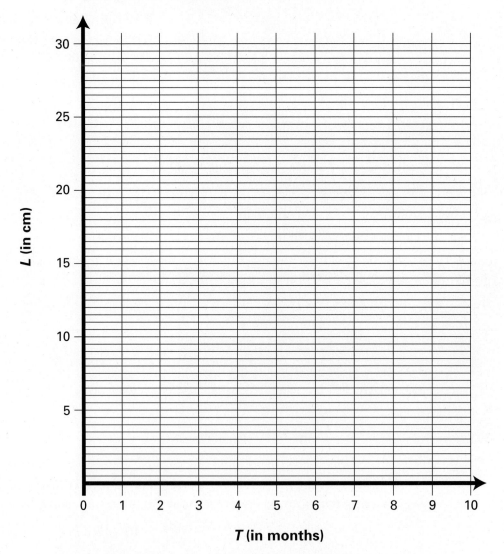

T (in months)

c. What will happen if you continue the graph? How do you know this? What will it look like in the table?

4. Reflect The formula used is a simplified model for hair growth. In reality, do you think hair will keep growing 1.5 cm per month over a very long period?

Here are some different formulas.

(1) *number of kilometers* = 1.6 × *number of miles*

(2) *saddle height* (in cm) = *inseam* (in cm) × 1.08

(3) *circumference* = 3.14 × *diameter*

(4) *area* = 3.14 × *radius*²

(5) *F* = 32 + 1.8 × *C*

Here is an explanation for each formula.

Formula (1) is a conversion rule to change miles into kilometers (km).

Formula (2) gives the relationship between the saddle height of a bicycle and the inseam of your jeans.

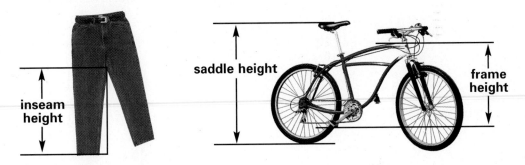

Formula (3) describes the relationship between the diameter of a circle and its circumference.

Formula (4) describes the relationship between the area of a circle and its radius.

Formula (5) is a conversion rule to change degrees Celsius into degrees Fahrenheit.

Use the formulas to answer these questions.

5. a. About how many kilometers is a 50-mile journey?

   b. A marathon race is a little bit more than 42 km.

   About how many miles long is a marathon race?

6. If the temperature is 25°C, should you wear a warm woolen jacket?

7. Compute the circumference and the area of a circle with a diameter of 10 cm.

8. Explain why it would not be sensible to compute:
saddle height = 30 × 1.08 = 33.

You can abbreviate rules and formulas using symbols instead of words as is done in formula (5). For instance a short version of formula (1) is: $K = 1.6 \times M$.

9. **a.** Rewrite formulas (2), (3) and (4) in a shortened way.

   b. One formula is mathematically different from the others. Which one do you think it is and why?

Linear Relationships

If we just look at a formula or a graph and we are not interested in the context it represents, we can use a general form.

Remember: In a coordinate system the **horizontal** axis is called the **x-axis** and the **vertical** one is called the **y-axis**.

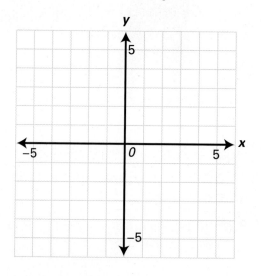

In the general x-y-form, rule (1)

$$\text{number of kilometers} = 1.6 \times \text{number of miles}$$

is written as $y = 1.6\,x$.

10. Rewrite the formulas (2), (3), (4), and (5) in the general form, using the symbols x and y.

The four formulas (1), (2), (3), and (5) represent relationships of the same kind. These are called **linear relationships**. Graphs representing linear relationships will always be **straight lines**.

11. Use **Student Activity Sheet 1** to make a graph of the relationship between the area and the radius of a circle. Is this relationship linear? Why or why not?

The formula corresponding to a straight line is known as an **equation of the line**.

Look at the equation $y = -4 + 2x$.

12. a. Complete the table and draw a graph. Be sure to use both positive and negative numbers in your coordinate system.

x	y
−2	−8
−1	
0	
1	
2	

b. This is another equation: $y = 2(x - 2)$.

Do you think the corresponding graph will be different from the graph of $y = -4 + 2x$? Explain your answer.

c. Reflect Suppose that the line representing the formula $y = 1.6x$ is drawn in the same coordinate system. Is this line steeper or less steep than the graph of $y = -4 + 2x$? Explain how you know.

The Slope of a Line

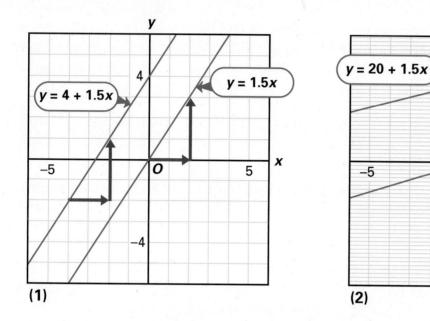

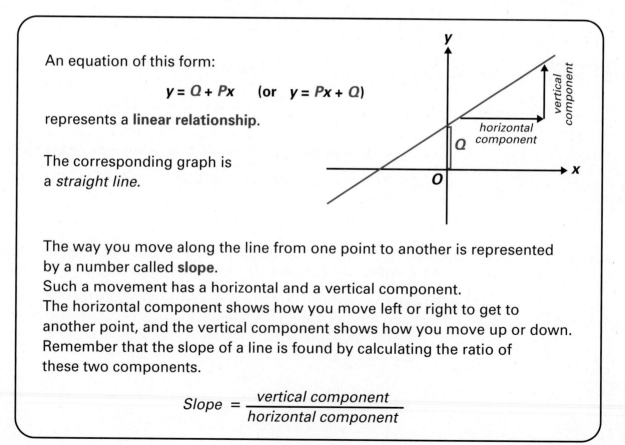

(1)

(2)

13. Each graph shows two linear relationships. How are these alike? How are they different?

An equation of this form:

$$y = Q + Px \quad \text{(or} \quad y = Px + Q\text{)}$$

represents a **linear relationship**.

The corresponding graph is a *straight line*.

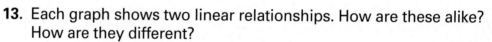

The way you move along the line from one point to another is represented by a number called **slope**.
Such a movement has a horizontal and a vertical component.
The horizontal component shows how you move left or right to get to another point, and the vertical component shows how you move up or down.
Remember that the slope of a line is found by calculating the ratio of these two components.

$$Slope = \frac{vertical\ component}{horizontal\ component}$$

14. a. What is the slope of each of the lines in picture **(1)** on the previous page? In picture **(2)**?

b. Suppose you were going to draw a line in picture **(2)** that was midway between the two lines in the graph. Give the equation for your line.

15. Patty wants to draw the graph for the equation $y = 20 + 1.5x$ in picture **(1)**. Why is this not a very good plan?

To draw the graphs of $y = 1.5x$ and $y = 20 + 1.5x$ in one picture, you can use a coordinate system with different scales on the two axes. This is shown in picture **(2)**. The lines in **(2)** have the *same slope* as the lines in **(1)**, although they look less steep in the picture!

16. Below you see three tables corresponding with three linear relationships.

x	y
−4	−7
−2	−1
0	5
2	11
4	17

x	y
−10	8
−5	4
0	0
5	−4
10	−8

x	y
−20	6
−10	6
0	6
10	6
20	6

a. How can you see that each table fits a linear relationship?

b. Each table corresponds to a graph. Find the slope of each graph.

Intercepts on the Axes

17. a. Draw and label a line that intersects the *y*-axis at (0, 3) and that has a slope of $\frac{1}{3}$.

b. Do the same for the line going through (0, 3) but with a slope of $-\frac{1}{3}$.

c. Describe how the two lines seem to be related.

d. At what points do the lines intersect the *x*-axis?

In the graph you see that the line corresponding to $y = 5 - 2x$ intersects the *y*-axis at (0, 5) and the *x*-axis at $(2\frac{1}{2}, 0)$.

These points can be described as follows:

- The **y-intercept** of the graph is 5.

- The **x-intercept** of the graph is $2\frac{1}{2}$.

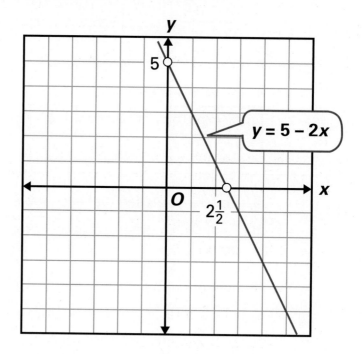

The next graph has two red points from a line. Try to answer the following questions without drawing that line.

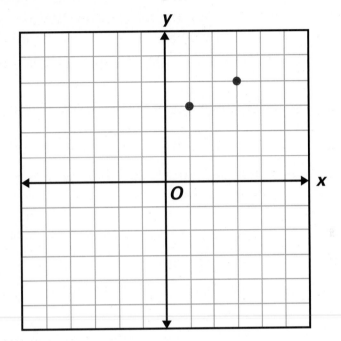

18. **a.** What is the slope of the line?

 b. What is the *y*-intercept?

 c. What is the *x*-intercept?

19. Determine the slope, the *y*-intercept, and the *x*-intercept of the graphs corresponding to the following equations. Explain how you did each problem.

 a. $y = 5 + 2x$

 b. $y = 4 - 8x$

 c. $y = 4x - 6$

 d. $y = -1\frac{1}{2}x - 4\frac{1}{2}$

20. Find an equation of the straight line

 a. with *y*-intercept 1 and slope 2;

 b. with *x*-intercept 2 and slope 1;

 c. with *x*-intercept 2 and *y*-intercept 1.

 Explain what you did to find the equation in each case.

21. **a.** A line has slope 8 and *y*-intercept 320. Determine the *x*-intercept.

 b. Another line has slope −8 and *x*-intercept 5. Determine the *y*-intercept.

Summary

A formula of this form represents a **linear relationship**.

$$y = Q + Px \quad \text{or} \quad y = Px + Q$$

The corresponding graph is a **straight line** with slope *P* and *y-intercept Q*.

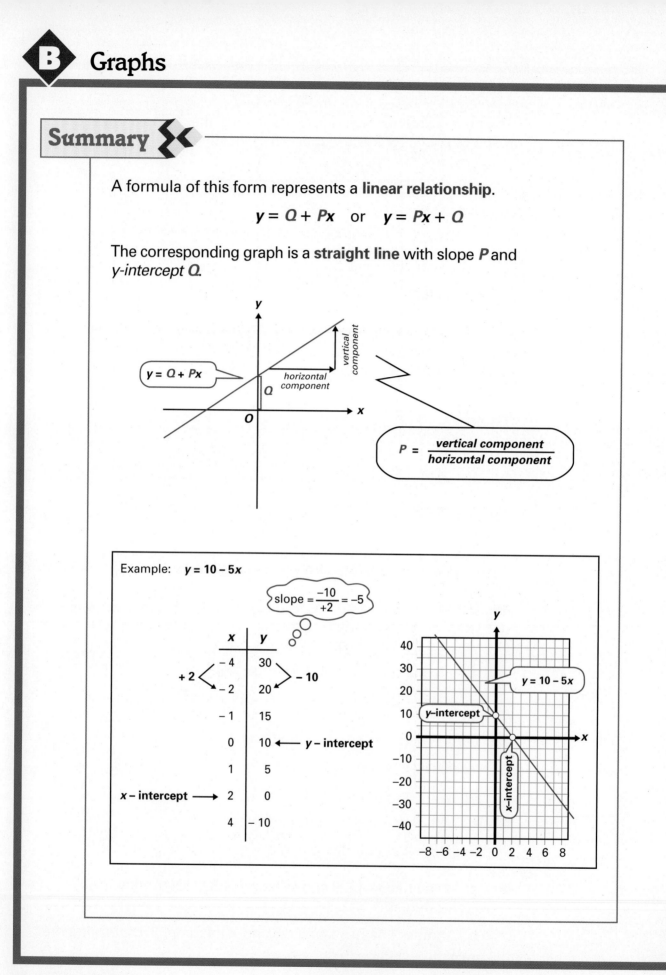

$$P = \frac{\text{vertical component}}{\text{horizontal component}}$$

Example: $y = 10 - 5x$

$$\text{slope} = \frac{-10}{+2} = -5$$

x	y
−4	30
−2	20
−1	15
0	10 ← *y* – intercept
1	5
2	0
4	−10

+2, −10

x – intercept → 2

$y = 10 - 5x$

y–intercept

x–intercept

Check Your Work

1. **a.** Draw the graphs corresponding to the formulas below in one coordinate system.

    $$y = 0.6x \quad y = 0.6x + 6 \quad y = 0.6x - 3$$

    b. Give the *y*-intercept of each graph.

    c. Give the *x*-intercept of each graph.

2. Here are four graphs and four equations. Which equation fits with which graph? Give both the letter of the graph and the number of the equation in your answer.

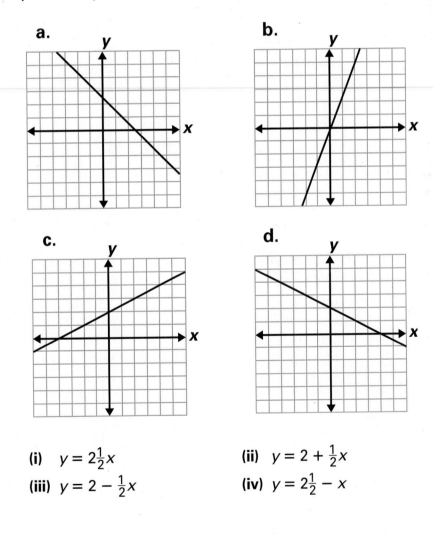

(i) $y = 2\frac{1}{2}x$

(iii) $y = 2 - \frac{1}{2}x$

(ii) $y = 2 + \frac{1}{2}x$

(iv) $y = 2\frac{1}{2} - x$

A 20-cm long candle is lighted.

The relationship between the length **L** (in centimeters) of this candle and the burning time **t** (in hours) is a linear relationship. The table corresponds to this relationship.

3. a. Use **Student Activity Sheet 2** to complete the table.

t (in hr)	0	1	2	3	4	5	6	7	8	9	10
L (in cm)	20					10					0

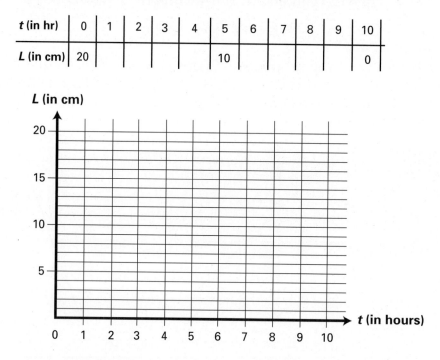

b. Use **Student Activity Sheet 2** to draw the graph corresponding to this relationship.

c. Give a formula representing the relationship between **t** and **L**.

For Further Reflection

Explain how you know a relationship is not linear.

Operations with Graphs

Numbers of Students

The graph below shows the number of students on September 1 at Rydell Middle School during the period 1996–2004.

1. The graph shows that the number of female students is increasing every year. What about the number of male students?

2. In which year was the number of girls in Rydell Middle School equal to the number of boys?

Students at Rydell Middle School

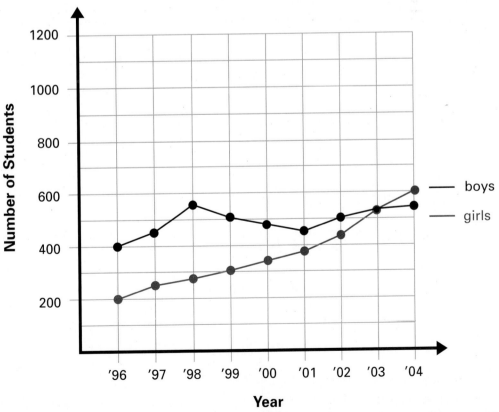

3. **a.** Use **Student Activity Sheet 2** to graph the total number of students in Rydell Middle School.

   b. Label the graph of the number of girls with **G** and that of the number of boys with **B**.

   c. How can you label the graph of the total number of students using the letters **G** and **B**?

Adding Graphs

In airports and big buildings you sometimes see a moving walkway. The speed of such a walkway is usually about six kilometers per hour. Some people stand on a walkway; others walk on it.

4. Suppose the length of the walkway is 50 meters, and you stand on it from the start. How long does it take you to reach the other end?

5. On **Student Activity Sheet 3** fill in the table for "walkway" and draw the graph that shows the relationship between *distance* covered (in meters) and *time* (in seconds). Label your graph with **M**.

6. **a.** Find a word formula that fits the graph and the table you just made.

   Write your answer as **distance** = ...

   b. Write your formula in the general form y = ...

Some people prefer to walk beside the walkway, because they do not like the moving "floor."

7. Answer questions 4, 5, and 6 for a person who walks 50 meters next to the walkway at a regular pace with a speed of four kilometers per hour. Draw the graph in the same coordinate system and label this graph with **W**.

8. **a.** Now add the two graphs to make a new one, labeled **M + W**. You may use the last part of the table on **Student Activity Sheet 3** if you want to.

   b. Give a formula that fits the graph **M + W**.

   c. What does the new graph **M + W** represent?

   d. What is the slope of each of the lines **M, W,** and **M + W**? What does the slope tell you about the speed?

In the following exercises, it is not necessary to know what the graphs represent.

Here are two graphs, indicated by **A** and **B**.

From these two graphs, you can make the "sum graph," **A + B**.

The point (2, 7) of this sum graph is already plotted.

9. **a.** Explain why the point (2, 7) is on the sum graph.

   b. Use **Student Activity Sheet 4** to draw the graph **A + B**. Make sure to label this graph.

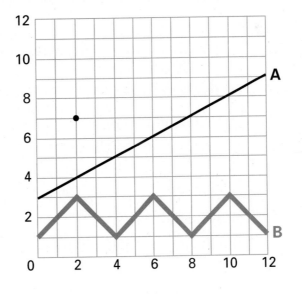

A graph is multiplied by 2, for instance, by multiplying the height of every point by 2.

10. Use **Student Activity Sheet 4** to draw the graph of **2B** and label it.

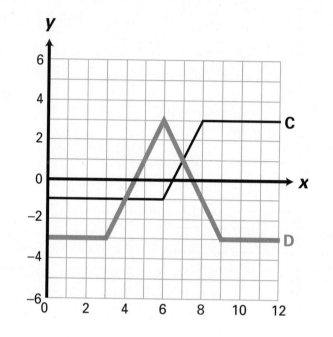

11. a. Use **Student Activity Sheet 4** to draw the graph **C + D** and label this graph.

 b. Draw the graph of $\frac{1}{2}$(**C + D**) and label this as **M**.

 c. The graph **M** goes through the intersection point of **C** and **D**. How could you have known this without looking at the sum graph, **C + D**?

12. Create two graphs and design a problem about operating with these graphs.

Operating with Graphs and Expressions

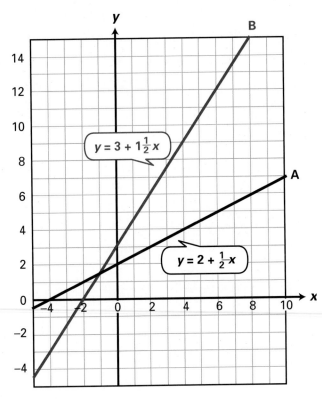

Consider two graphs that represent linear relationships.

Graph **A** corresponds to $y = 2 + \frac{1}{2}x$.

Graph **B** corresponds to $y = 3 + 1\frac{1}{2}x$.

13. **a.** Use **Student Activity Sheet 5** to draw the graph **A + B**.

   b. Write an equation to represent the graph **A + B**.

14. **a.** Use **Student Activity Sheet 5** to draw the graph **B − A**.

   b. Write an equation to represent the graph **B − A**.

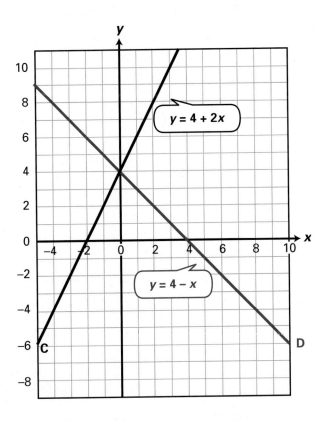

Graph **C** corresponds to $y = 4 + 2x$.

Graph **D** corresponds to $y = 4 - x$.

15. **a.** Use **Student Activity Sheet 5** to draw the graph **C + D**.

   b. Write an equation that corresponds to graph **C + D**.

16. **a.** Use **Student Activity Sheet 5** to draw the graphs $\frac{1}{2}$**C** and $\frac{1}{2}$**D**.

   b. Write an equation that corresponds to graph $\frac{1}{2}$**C**.

   Write an equation that corresponds to graph $\frac{1}{2}$**D**.

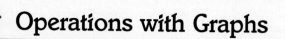

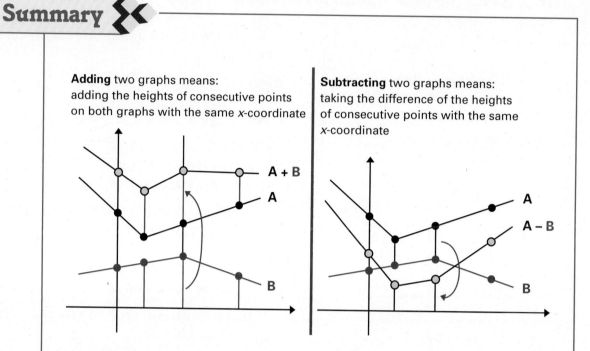

Adding two graphs means:
adding the heights of consecutive points on both graphs with the same x-coordinate

Subtracting two graphs means:
taking the difference of the heights of consecutive points with the same x-coordinate

If you add or subtract two graphs, the corresponding expressions are also added or subtracted.

Example:
If graph **A** corresponds to $y = 5 + 0.75x$ and graph **B** to $y = -2 + 0.5x$, then graph **A + B** corresponds to $y = 3 + 1.25x$ and graph **A − B** to $y = 7 + 0.25x$.

Multiplying a graph by a fixed number means:
multiplying the height of every point of the graph by that number.

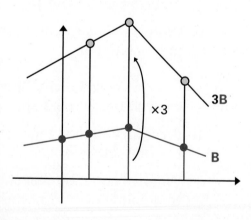

If you multiply a graph by a number, the corresponding expression is multiplied by that number.

Example:

If graph **B** corresponds to $y = -2 + 0.5x$, then graph **3B** corresponds to $y = -6 + 1.5x$.

Graphs **A** and **B** are shown in the picture.

1. a. Copy this picture and then draw the graph **A + B**.

  b. Make a new copy of the picture and draw the graphs
    2A and $\frac{2}{3}$**B**. Label your graphs.

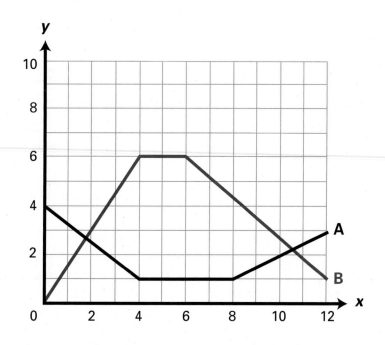

C is the graph corresponding to $y = 3 + x$.

D is the graph corresponding to $y = 1 - 3x$.

2. a. Draw **C** and **D** in one coordinate system.

  b. Draw the graphs of **C + D** and **C − D**.

  c. Write the equations corresponding to **C + D** and **C − D**.

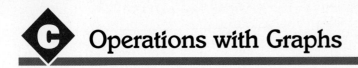
In the picture you see the graphs **A** of $y = \frac{1}{2}x$, **B** of $y = 3$, and **C** of $y = x + 3$.

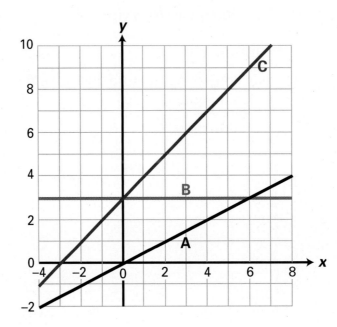

3. **a.** Copy this picture and draw the graphs **A** + **B** and $\frac{1}{2}$**C** in the same coordinate system.

   b. If you did your work correctly, you see that the graph **A** + **B** is above the graph $\frac{1}{2}$**C**.

     How can you explain this by using the equations corresponding to **A** + **B** and $\frac{1}{2}$**C**?

For Further Reflection

Describe in your own words the relationship between a graph and any multiple of the graph. Include intersects, slope, and height, and also make sure you include both positive and negative multiples.

D Equations to Solve

Finding the Unknown

If $x = ?$, then $20 + 5x = 50$

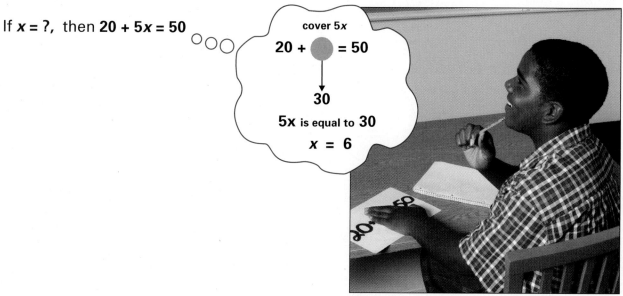

cover $5x$

$20 + \bigcirc = 50$

30

$5x$ is equal to 30

$x = 6$

1. Look at the "cover method" above and find the value of x.

If $x = \ldots\ldots$, then $20 + 5x = 35$

If $x = \ldots\ldots$, then $20 - 5x = 10$

If $x = \ldots\ldots$, then $20 - 5x = 0$

If $x = \ldots\ldots$, then $6(x + 5) = -60$

If $x = \ldots\ldots$, then $6(x - 5) = 60$

If $x = \ldots\ldots$, then $6(x - 5) = 0$

If $x = \ldots\ldots$, then $\dfrac{30}{x + 2} = 10$

If $x = \ldots\ldots$, then $\dfrac{30}{x - 2} = -10$

2. Find the values of *a, b, c, d, e, f, g,* and *h* that make each of the equations true.

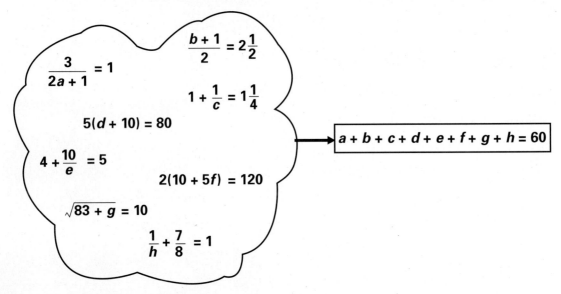

$$\frac{3}{2a + 1} = 1$$

$$\frac{b + 1}{2} = 2\frac{1}{2}$$

$$1 + \frac{1}{c} = 1\frac{1}{4}$$

$$5(d + 10) = 80$$

$$4 + \frac{10}{e} = 5$$

$$2(10 + 5f) = 120$$

$$\sqrt{83 + g} = 10$$

$$\frac{1}{h} + \frac{7}{8} = 1$$

$$a + b + c + d + e + f + g + h = 60$$

Two Arithmetic Sequences

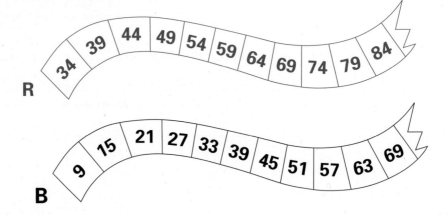

R   34 39 44 49 54 59 64 69 74 79 84

B   9 15 21 27 33 39 45 51 57 63 69

The numbers in both strips form an arithmetic sequence. If you compare the corresponding numbers in pairs, you see that the red numbers in **R** are greater than the black numbers in **B**: 34 > 9, 39 > 15, 44 > 21, etc.

3. **Reflect** If you continue both strips as far as you want, will this always be true? Why or why not?

Sarah says: "After many steps in both strips you will find a number in **R** that is equal to its corresponding number in **B**."

4. Do you agree with Sarah? If your answer is yes, after how many steps will that be?

5. a. Make a strip of the differences between the red and black numbers of **R** and **B**.

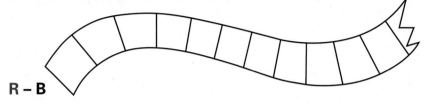

R − B

b. If you continue this strip as far as you want, will there be negative numbers in the strip?

c. After how many steps will the number strip show 0?

d. How can this strip help you to solve problem 4?

You see a subtraction of two number strips.

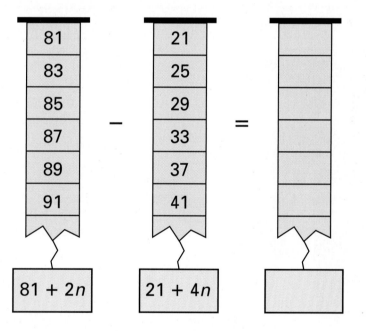

6. a. Fill in the missing numbers and the expression for the strip of differences.

b. After how many steps will the number in the last strip be 0?

c. For which value of n is $81 + 2n$ equal to $21 + 4n$?

Jess is a handyman who does many jobs for people.

He calculates the price (in $) for a job by using the formula:

$$P = 30 + 60 \times H$$

7. a. What do you think **P** means? And **H**?

b. What is the meaning of each of the numbers in the formula?

Barrie lives in the same town, and she also does different jobs for people.

To compete with Jess, she charges $45 per working hour and $75 as a service charge for coming to the site.

8. a. What is Barrie's formula to calculate the price of a job?

b. On **Student Activity Sheet 6** draw the graphs for both formulas and label your graphs with **J** and **B**.

c. What does the intersection point of both graphs represent?

d. Draw the graph **B−J**. What is the formula corresponding to this graph?

■ **e. Reflect** Barrie claims that she is less expensive than Jess, since she only charges $45 an hour. What is your comment?

Solving Equations

In the first two problems of this section you solved equations with the cover method. This method cannot always be used.

Sarah's assertion (problem 4) for instance, may lead to an equation with the *unknown* on both sides. Her assertion can be expressed as:

There is a value of n for which $34 + 5n$ is equal to $9 + 6n$.

To investigate if Sarah is right, you solve the equation

$$34 + 5n = 9 + 6n$$

In that case you cannot start with the cover method!
Two possible strategies to solve this problem are:

Balance Method
(Remember the frogs in *Graphing Equations*.)

$$-9 \left(\begin{array}{c} 34 + 5n = 9 + 6n \\ 25 + 5n = 6n \\ 25 = n \end{array} \right) \begin{array}{c} -9 \\ -5n \end{array}$$

$-5n$

$n = 25$

Difference-is-0 Method (Calculate the difference of both sides and let this be 0.)

$$34 + 5n = 9 + 6n$$

$$34 + 5n$$
$$\underline{-\quad 9 + 6n}$$
$$25 - n = 0$$

9. **a.** Solve the equation $30 + 60H = 75 + 45H$ using the balance method and the difference-is-0 method.

   b. What does the solution mean for Jess and Barrie?

10. Solve each of the following equations. Use each method at least once.

    a. $10 - x = -8 + 2x$ **b.** $10 - x = 4x - 20$ **c.** $4x - 20 = -8 + 2x$

11. Create an equation with the unknown on both sides. The solution has to be equal to your age.

12. **Reflect** What happens if you use the difference-is-0 method to solve:

$$3 + 5p = 5p$$

What conclusion can you make?

Intersecting Graphs

The three graphs are drawn in the same coordinate system.

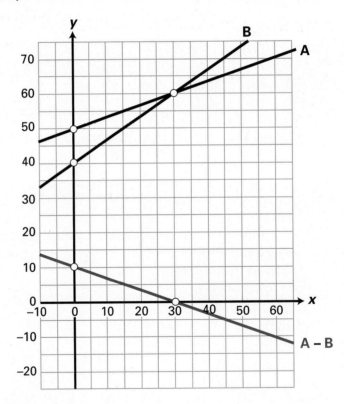

13. The red graph is the "difference graph" of **A** and **B**

a. How can you see that in the picture?

b. Give equations corresponding to the graphs **A**, **B**, and **A − B**.

c. What is the *x*-intercept of the red graph?

d. What are the coordinates of the intersection point of **A** and **B**?

14. a. In one coordinate system, draw the lines corresponding to the equations:

$$y = 32 - 4x \text{ and } y = 8(6 - x)$$

b. Calculate the slope, the *y*-intercept, and the *x*-intercept of both lines.

c. The two lines have an intersection point. Find the coordinates of this point.

15. a. Use **Student Activity Sheet 6** and draw the graphs corresponding to

$$y = 2 + 4x \text{ and } y = -6 + 3x$$

b. Should the graphs intersect if the grid is extended far enough?

If you think yes, calculate the intersection point.

If you think no, explain why you are sure they will never intersect.

Now look at the graphs **A** and **B**.

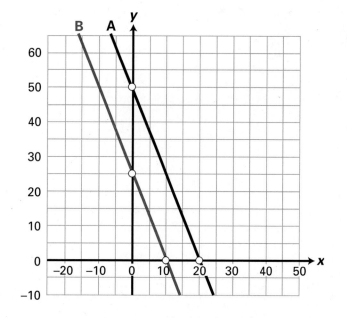

16. a. How can you know for sure that the graphs **A** and **B** will not intersect, not even if the grid is extended?

b. Reflect What special property does the difference graph **A − B** have?

D Equations to solve

Summary

In this section you have seen some methods to solve an *equation* with one *unknown.*

The first method may be called the cover method.

Two examples:

$$9 \times (5 + x) = 72 \qquad \text{and} \qquad 9 + 4x = 81$$

In the first equation you can cover the expression **5 + x**

In the second equation you can cover the expression **4x**

That leads to:

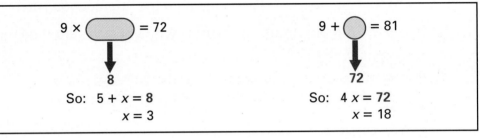

The cover method does not work if the unknown appears on both sides of the equation.

Look at the equation $98 - 5x = -1 + 4x$.

The unknown **x** is on both sides.

You can apply the method of performing the same operation on both sides.

Another good way is to use the difference-is-0 method.

$98 - 5x = -1 + 4x$ $\Big)$ add 1	$98 - 5x = -1 + 4x$
$99 - 5x = 4x$ $\Big)$ add 5x	$98 - 5x$
$99 = 9x$	$-\ \underline{-1 + 4x}$
$x = 11$	$\overline{99 - 9x = 0}$
	$x = 11$

You can find the intersection point of two graphs by solving an equation.

Example:

The graphs with equations $y = 300 + 65x$ and $y = 150 + 80x$ have an intersection point because the slopes are different.

The x-coordinate of the intersection point is found by solving:

$300 + 65x = 150 + 80x$ or $150 - 15x = 0$

The solution is $x = 10$, and the intersection point is $(10, 950)$.

Check Your Work

1. Solve the following equations with the cover method.

   a. $99 + 2x = 100$ c. $\frac{99}{2x} = 11$

   b. $9(x + 4) = 99$ d. $\frac{x + 9}{4} = 25$

2. Design an equation that can be solved using the difference-is-0 method.

3. a. Draw the graphs corresponding to $y = 7 - 3x$ and $y = 2x - 1$ in one coordinate system.

   b. Calculate the x-coordinate of the intersection point for the graphs.

4. Do the graphs of $y = 40 + 8x$ and $y = 8(x - 7)$ have an intersection point? Why or why not?

For Further Reflection

Is it possible to have two different lines that intersect at more than one point? Explain.

E

Operating with Lengths and Areas

Crown Town

Here is a map of a district in Crown Town. The map shows the route of a bus with six stops.

Stop 1 is the beginning and ending of the route.

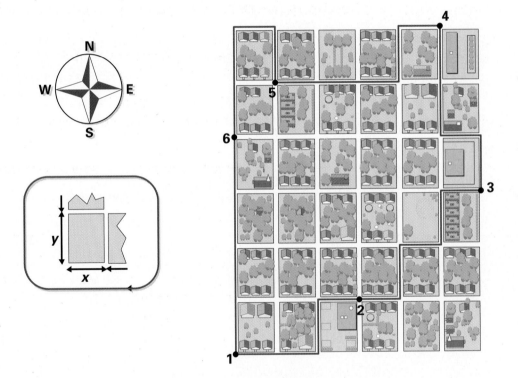

The streets run east-west, the avenues north-south.

The lengths of the streets and the avenues are not given until further notice.

The length of a part of a street along one block is represented by *x*.

The length of a part of an avenue along one block is represented by *y*.

The length of the route of the bus from stop to stop can be represented by an expression.

For instance: Route 1 → 2 can be represented by $3x + y$.

1. a. Find expressions for the routes.

Route 1 → 2 ....

Route 2 → 3 ....

Route 3 → 4 ....

Route 4 → 5 ....

Route 5 → 6 ....

Route 6 → 1 ....

b. Which two routes must be equal in length?

Here is some information about the lengths of the streets and the avenues: four streets have the same length as three of the avenues, for short, $4x = 3y$.

2. Reflect Are there other routes that you are sure have the same length? Which ones and how can you be sure?

To find out the lengths of the streets and the avenues you need the following information: The route from stop 5 to stop 6 is 1,200 meters.

3. Calculate the length of one complete bus trip from the starting point to the end.

Perimeters

Two squares with one rectangle in between them are shown.

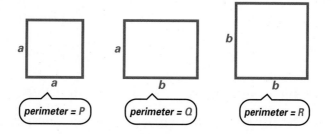

4. a. For the perimeter **P** of the square with side **a**, the formula is **P** = 4**a**. Explain this formula.

b. Give formulas for the perimeters **Q** and **R**.

c. **P**, **Q**, and **R** have the following relationship.

$Q = \frac{1}{2}P + \frac{1}{2}R$. How can you explain this formula?

Next you see three hexagons with six equal angles.

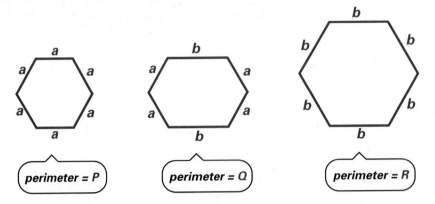

perimeter = P   perimeter = Q   perimeter = R

5. a. Find formulas for the perimeters **P, Q,** and **R.**

b. Find a formula for **Q** in terms of **P** and **R.**

c. Design a hexagon with equal angles and perimeter **S** in such a way that $S = \frac{1}{3}P + \frac{2}{3}R.$

Cross Figures

This is a cross figure. The sum of the lengths **x** and **y** is 12 cm.

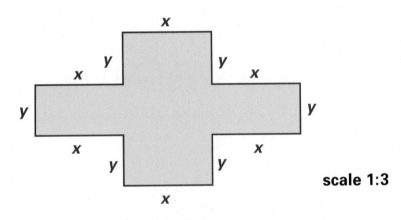

scale 1:3

There are many cross figures with the property $x + y = 12$.

6. Draw two other cross figures with $x + y = 12$ (scale 1:3).

7. All such cross figures have the same perimeter. How many centimeters are in the perimeter?

Now you will learn about the areas of different cross figures.

The table has been partly filled; the sum of x and y in each row has to be 12.

A represents the area of the corresponding cross figure.

8. a. Copy the table and fill in the missing numbers.

   b. You can continue the table with $x = 8, 9$, etc. Does that make much sense? Why?

x (in cm)	y (in cm)	A (in cm²)
1	11	55
2	10	100
3	9	
4		
5		
6		
7		
…….		

9. a. What is special about the shape of the cross figure in the table with the biggest area?

   b. Use the drawing of the cross figure to explain the formula $A = 5xy$.

Formulas for Perimeters and Areas

10. Find formulas for the perimeter and the area of each of the figures.

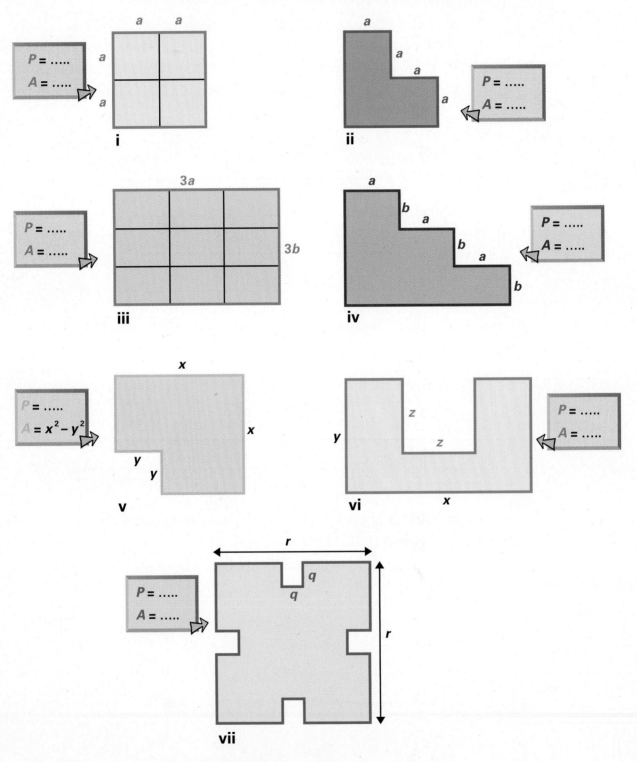

11. Design a figure with area $A = x^2 + 4y^2$ and perimeter $P = 4x + 8y$.

Equivalent Expressions

$10a + 10b$ is equivalent to $10(a + b)$.

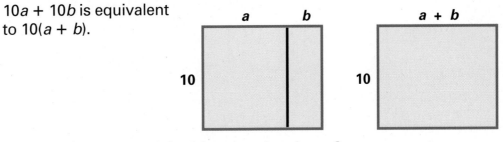

12. How can you explain this using the picture?

13. Find equivalent expressions using the pictures.

a. $15x + 15y =$ ....

b.   ....

c.   ....

d.   ....

e.   ....

f.   ....

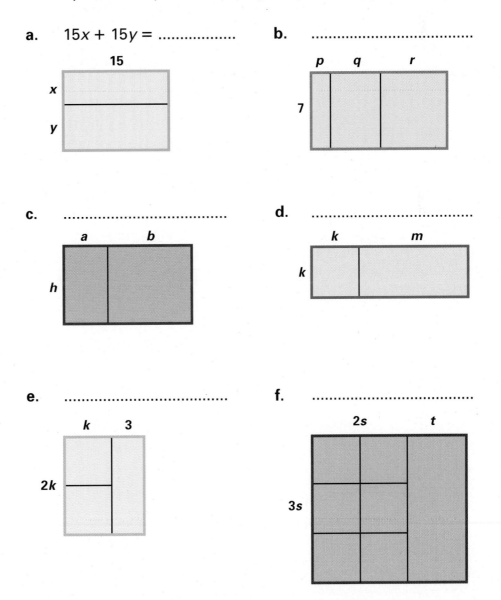

The Distribution Rule

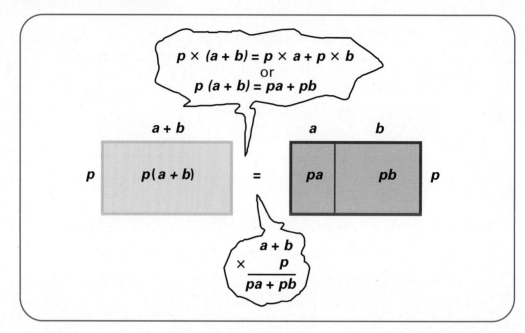

14. Draw a picture to demonstrate that the expressions are equivalent.

    a. $a(k + m + n)$ and $ak + am + an$

    b. $3(2x + y)$ and $6x + 3y$

15. Calculate $ax + ay$ if $a = 25$ and $x + y = 12$.

16. Right or wrong? Explain your answer.

    a. $6(a + 5b) \overset{?}{=} 6a + 5b$ **c.** $p(q + 8) \overset{?}{=} pq + 8p$

    b. $6(x + 5y) \overset{?}{=} 6x + 30y$ **d.** $uw + vw \overset{?}{=} (u + v)w$

17. Find the missing expressions in the tree.

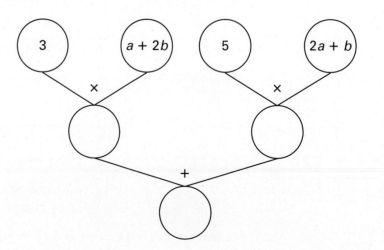

18. a. Give an expression for the length of the segment labeled by **?**.

b. Explain from the picture that $m(x - y)$ and $mx - my$ are equivalent expressions.

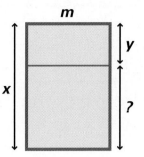

19. Create two equivalent expressions and make a corresponding picture.

Remarkable or Not?

For problems 20–22, a and b are positive integers with the sum 10.

S is the sum of the squares of a and b, so $S = a^2 + b^2$.

T is the sum of ab and ba, so $T = ab + ba$.

20. Which values can **S** have? And **T**? Copy and complete the table.

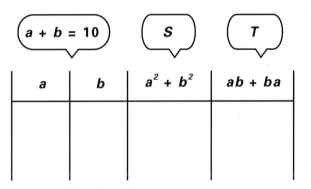

a	b	$a^2 + b^2$	$ab + ba$

21. a. Calculate the sum $S + T$. What did you discover?

b. Reflect Investigate what happens with $S + T$ if a and b are decimal numbers whose sum is 10, for example, $a = 3.8$ and $b = 6.2$.

Investigate some other examples. What did you find?

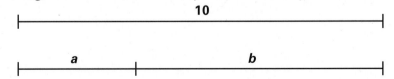

22. a. Draw a square with side a and one with side b.

b. Draw a rectangle with horizontal side a and vertical side b and draw one with horizontal side b and vertical side a.

c. How can you explain that $S + T = 100$?

Look at the two expressions.

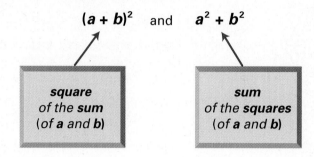

$(a + b)^2$ and $a^2 + b^2$

square
of the **sum**
(of **a** and **b**)

sum
of the **squares**
(of **a** and **b**)

23. Are the expressions equivalent? Why or why not?

24. *Smart arithmetic*: Use the picture to calculate $a^2 + 2ab + b^2$
for $a = 63$ and $b = 37$.

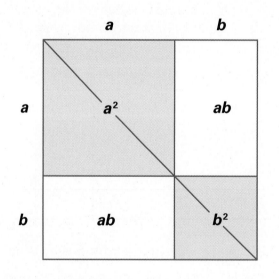

Math History

Euclid (ca.330–275 B.C.)

Euclid, the Greek mathematician, is probably the most famous math teacher of all times. He wrote a book titled *The Elements* about geometry and numbers. It was the principal geometry text for about 2,000 years.

Look at proposition 4 of Book 2 of *The Elements*. Translated from Greek it says:

> *If a straight line be cut at random, the square on the whole is equal to the squares on the segments and twice the rectangle contained by the segments.*

Look at Euclid's illustration of this proposition.

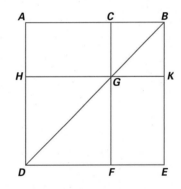

The straight line is the segment *AB* which is cut at *C*.

The square on the whole is *ABED*.

The lines *HK* and *CF*, which are parallel to *AB* and *AD* respectively, intersect the diagonal *DB* at the same point (*G*).

Now you can understand that the squares on the segments *AC* and *BC* are equal to the squares *DFGH* and *BCGK*. You can also see that the rectangle contained by the segments *AC* and *BC* is equal to each of the rectangles *ACGH* and *EFGK*.

The area of *ABED* is equal to the sum of the areas of the squares *DFGH* and *BCGK* and the rectangles *ACGH* and *EFGK*.

Compare this with the problems on pages 49 and 50.

Euclid's proposition later became one of the main rules in algebra:

$$(p + q)^2 = p^2 + q^2 + 2pq$$

E Operating with Lengths and Areas

Summary

In this section you have investigated formulas for perimeters and areas of plane figures.

Two examples:

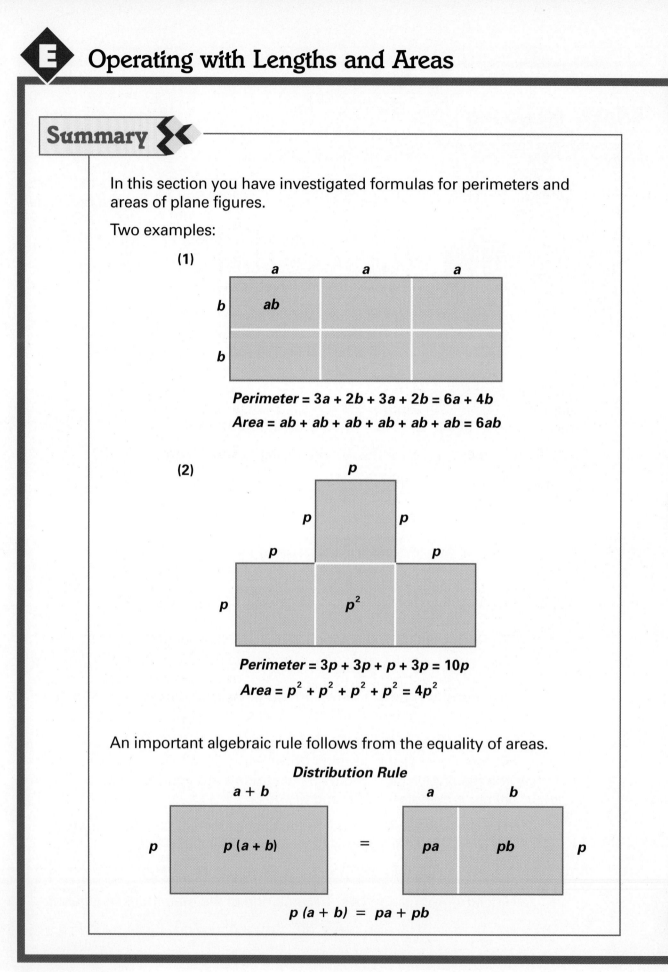

(1)

Perimeter = 3a + 2b + 3a + 2b = 6a + 4b

Area = ab + ab + ab + ab + ab + ab = 6ab

(2)

Perimeter = 3p + 3p + p + 3p = 10p

Area = $p^2 + p^2 + p^2 + p^2 = 4p^2$

An important algebraic rule follows from the equality of areas.

Distribution Rule

p (a + b) = pa + pb

Consider the following grid of rectangles with sides **h** and **v**.

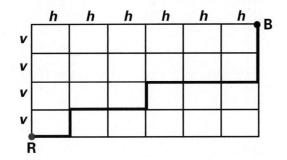

There are many "short routes" from point **R** to point **B** along the lines of the grid. One example of a short route is shown in the picture above.

1. Find an expression for the length of such a short route.

Consider the following three expressions:

$$(v + v + v + v) \times (h + h + h + h + h + h);$$

$$4v \times 6h;$$

$$10\,vh$$

2. a. Which of these expressions represents the area of the grid?

   b. Give another expression for this area.

   c. A rectangular part of the grid has the area **6vh**. The sides of this part are along the grid lines. Which expressions represent the sides of this part? (There are three possibilities!)

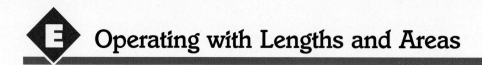
Look at both figures.

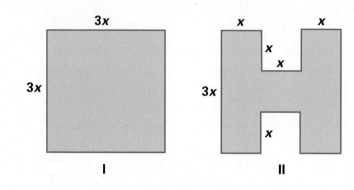

3. **a.** Figure I has a greater area than Figure II. Give an expression for the difference between those areas.

   b. Which of the two figures has the greater perimeter? Give an expression for that perimeter.

4. Rewrite the following expressions as short as possible.

   a. $3(2x + 4y + 5z) + 4(x + 2y + 6z)$

   b. $a(p + q) + a(p - q)$

For Further Reflection

Draw a figure that has the same area and perimeter. Explain how you know that the area and perimeter are the same.

Additional Practice

Section A Operating with Sequences

1. Find the missing expressions in the tree.

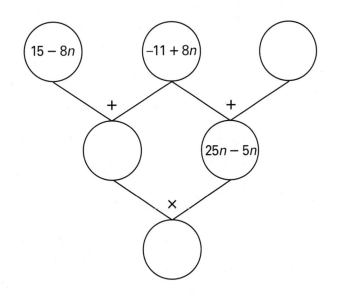

2. Rewrite the following expression to be as short as possible:

$3 \times (3 - 4n) + 4 \times (4 - 5n) + 5 \times (-5 + 6n)$

Olympic years are divisible by four.

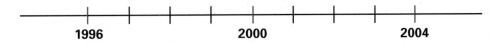

3. a. What expression can you use to represent an arbitrary Olympic year?

   b. Which Olympic year succeeds that year? Which Olympic year precedes it?

Olympic winter games are presently held in a year that falls exactly between two Olympic years.

   c. What expression can you use to represent an arbitrary year of winter games?

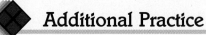

Section B Graphs

A linear relationship has a graph with *x*-intercept 75 and *y*-intercept 50.

1. a. What is the slope of the graph?

    b. What is the equation of this graph?

A line has the equation

$$y = -3(x - 33\tfrac{1}{3}).$$

2. a. You can find the *x*-intercept of the line without calculations. Explain how.

    b. Find the *y*-intercept of this line.

3. Investigate whether the three points (0, −5), (12, 19) and (15, 25) are on a straight line or not.

A new spool contains 100 m of cotton thread. If you want to know how many meters are left on a used spool, you can weigh the spool. A new spool weighs 50 grams, and a spool with 50 m of thread left weighs 30 grams.

4. a. Complete the table (**L** = length of the thread in meters, **W** = weight of the spool in grams) :

L	0	10	20	30	40	50	60	70	80	90	100
W						30					50

    b. Make a graph corresponding to the table.

    c. One spool that has been used weighs 25 grams. How many meters of thread are left on that spool?

    d. Give a formula for the relationship between **W** and **L**.

5. Draw a line for each of the equations. Calculate the slope, the *y*-intercept, and the *x*-intercept.

    a. $y = 3(2 - x)$

    b. $y = 2(x + 5)$

Section C Operations with Graphs

In the picture you see graph **B** and graph **A** + **B**.

1. Copy this picture and then draw graph **A**.

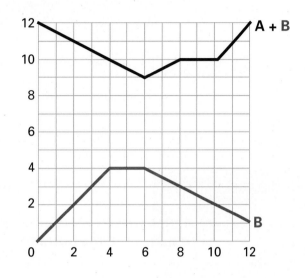

A straight line **A** passes through points (0, 4) and (6, 0) in a coordinate system.

Another straight line **B** is drawn in the same coordinate system and passes through points (0, 0) and (6, 12).

2. **a.** Draw both lines in a coordinate system and give the equation of each line.

   b. Draw the line that passes through (0, 4) and (6, 12). Explain why this line can be labeled as **A** + **B**.

A is the graph corresponding to $y = \frac{1}{2}x - 3$.

B is the graph corresponding to $y = -\frac{1}{3}x + 3$.

3. **a.** Draw both lines in one coordinate system.

   b. Draw the graph 2**A** + 3**B**. What is the corresponding equation of this graph?

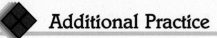
Section D Solving Equations

1. Use the cover method to solve the following equations.

    a. $76x + 203 = 279$

    b. $3(76 + x) = 240$

    c. $76 + \frac{6}{x} = 78$

    d. $\frac{76}{x-3} = 19$

2. Use the difference-is-0 method to solve the following equations.

    a. $5x + 90 = 10x - 10$

    b. $\frac{1}{2}x + 9 = x - 1$

    c. $24 - 3x = 56 - 7x$

    d. $3(2 + x) = 2(3 + x)$

Mr. Carlson wants to put a new roof on his house. Therefore, he has to buy new shingles. There are two construction firms in the region where he lives: Adams Company (AC) and Bishop Roofing Materials (BRM). They charge different prices.

- AC charges $ 0.75 per shingle and a $100 delivery fee.

- BRM charges $ 0.55 per shingle and a $200 delivery fee.

Mr. Carlson has calculated that it doesn't matter where he orders the shingles; the price offered by both firms will be the same.

3. How many shingles does Mr. Carlson want to order? Explain how you found your answer.

Two graphs represent linear relationships. The first graph (**A**) has x-intercept 5 and y-intercept 10. The second one (**B**) has x-intercept 10 and y-intercept 5.

4. **a.** Draw both graphs in one coordinate system.

    b. Find an equation that corresponds to **A**. What equation corresponds to **B**?

    c. Calculate the coordinates of the intersection point of both graphs.

Section **E** Operating with Lengths and Areas

Consider a cube with edge **a**.

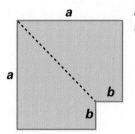

1. **a.** Write an expression for the total surface of this cube.

   b. Write an expression for the volume of this cube.

   Form a second cube with edges twice as long as the edges of the first one.

   c. Write expressions for the total area and for the volume of the second cube.

2. Rewrite each expression as short as possible.

   a. $6(x + 2y) + 5(y + 2z) + 4(z + 2x)$

   b. $7(5a + 3b + c) - 5(a + b + c)$

A small square, whose sides are of length **b**, is cut off from one corner of a larger square, whose sides are of length **a**.

3. **a.** Explain why an expression for the area of the remaining part (shaded) is

$$a^2 - b^2$$

You can divide the remaining figure in two equal parts by the dotted line. If you flip over one of the two parts, you can make a rectangle as shown.

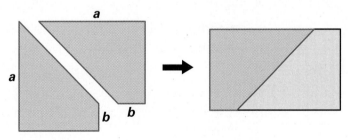

   b. The sides of the new rectangle are $a + b$ and $a - b$. Explain this.

   c. This is a famous algebra rule: $(a + b) \times (a - b) = a^2 - b^2$

   How can you explain this rule from the pictures above?

   d. *Mental arithmetic.* Use this rule to calculate
   31×29; 42×38; $6\frac{1}{2} \times 5\frac{1}{2}$.

Answers to Check Your Work

Section A Operating with Sequences

1.

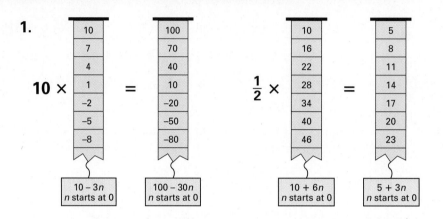

2. a. An arithmetic sequence will decrease if the growth step is negative, for example -3 in the expression $10 - 3n$.

b. If the growth step is 0, there is no increase and no decrease in the sequence since $0 \times n = 0$. All numbers in the sequence are equal to the start number.

3. If you made mistakes in these problems, try to do them again using number strips.

  a. $30 - 6n$ **b.** 3 **c.** $104 - 100n$

4. a. $1788 + 4n$, n starts at 0. Note that presidential elections take place every four years so the growth step is four.

b. 1960 was the year John F. Kennedy was elected President of the U.S. You might reason as follows: If 1960 was a presidential election year, there must be a value for n that makes

$$1788 + 4n = 1960$$

a true statement. To find such an n, you could guess and check: n would have to be bigger than 30 to get from 1788 to 1960, so try 35, etc. until you reached 43. You might also continue the sequence, but it would take a long time to write out all 43 terms.

Or you could argue that $1960 - 1788$ should be divisible by four.
$1960 - 1788 = 172$
$172 \div 4 = 43$
After 43 steps in the sequence, you will reach 1960.
$1788 + 4 \times 43 = 1960$

5. $2(6 - 3n) + (5 - 4n) = (12 - 6n) + (5 - 4n) = 17 - 10n$

Section B Graphs

1. a.

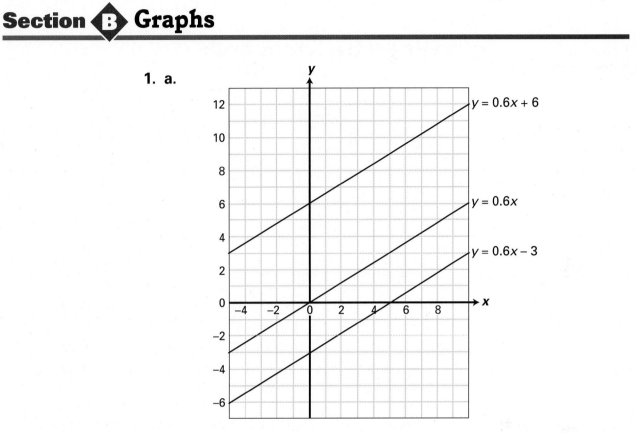

Note that your graphs need to be drawn in one coordinate system.

b.–c.

Formula	$y = 0.6x$	$y = 0.6x + 6$	$y = 0.6x - 3$
y-intercept	0	6	−3
x-intercept	0	−10	5

2. A − 4; B − 1; C − 2; D − 3

3. a.

t (in hr)	0	1	2	3	4	5	6	7	8	9	10
L (in cm)	20	18	16	14	12	10	8	6	4	2	0

Note that after five hours, the length of the candle decreased by 10 centimeters. Since this is a linear relationship, the decrease per hour is 10 ÷ 5 = 2.

3. b.

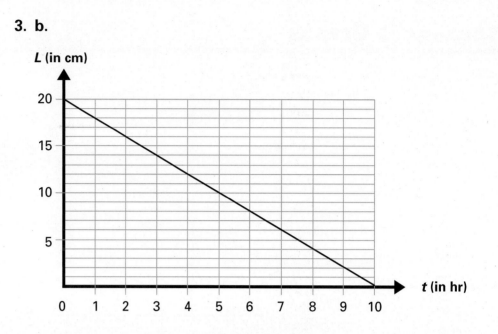

For this graph you only need positive numbers. Did you label your axes right?

  c. From the table, you can read the L-intercept. Remember that $t = 0$ for the L-intercept. For each increase of one of t, L decreases by two, thus, the slope is -2.

  Of course, you can also look at your graph to find the L-intercept and the slope.

  An equation of the line is $L = 20 - 2t$

Section ◈ Operations with Graphs

1. a.

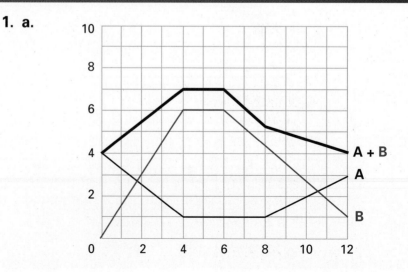

b.

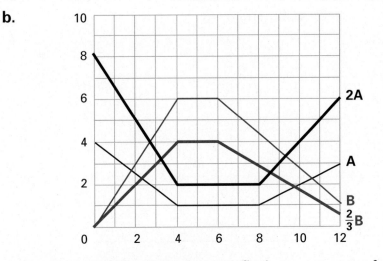

You may use a graphing calculator to find your answers for problems 2 and 3 if those are available.

2. **a.** Did you use a coordinate system with both positive and negative numbers? If nothing is known about the context of a formula, always use positive as well as negative numbers as shown in the graphs on the next page. You may always make a table first or you can use the *y*-intercept and the slope to help you draw the graph.

Graph A: The *y*-intercept is 3 and the slope is 1. Here is a sample table you can fill out and use.

x	−2	−1	0	1	2
y	1		3		

Graph B: The *y*-intercept is 1 and the slope is −3. Here is a sample table you can fill out and use.

x	−2	−1	0	1	2
y	7		1		

Did you label your graphs?

c. A + B corresponds to $y = (3 + x) + (1 − 3x) = 4 − 2x$.

A − B corresponds to $y = (3 + x) − (1 − 3x) = 2 + 4x$.

2. a., b., and **c.**   **3. a.**

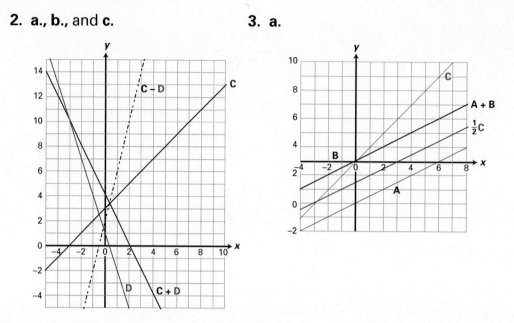

3. b. A + B corresponds to $y = \frac{1}{2}x + 3$.

$\frac{1}{2}$ C corresponds to $y = \frac{1}{2}(x + 3) = \frac{1}{2}x + 1\frac{1}{2}$.

The slopes of both lines are $\frac{1}{2}$, so the lines are parallel.

But a *y*-intercept of 3 is greater than the *y*-intercept $1\frac{1}{2}$.

Remember: You can write that in a short way as $3 > 1\frac{1}{2}$.

Thus, the graph for A + B is above the graph of $\frac{1}{2}$C.

Section Ⓓ Equations to Solve

1. a. $99 + 1 = 100$ so $2x = 1$, and $x = \frac{1}{2}$.

   b. $9 \times 11 = 99$ so $(x + 4) = 11$; $x = 7$.

   c. 99 divided by 9 is 11 so $2x = 9$; $x = 4.5$ or $4\frac{1}{2}$.

   d. 100 divided by 4 is 25, so $(x + 9) = 100$ and $x = 91$.

2. Discuss your problem and its solution with a classmate. Check the answer by filling in the value for *x* you found. Look at the summary for an example.

3. a.

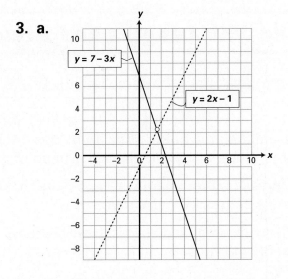

b. The *x*-coordinate of the intersection point can be found by solving the equation: $7 - 3x = 2x - 1$

The cover method does not work here. You can choose to perform the same operation on both sides or you can use the difference-is-0 method. Both solutions are shown here. Of course you need to use only the one you like best.

$7 - 3x = 2x - 1$ Add $3x$	$7 - 3x = 2x - 1$
$7 = 5x - 1$ Add 1	$7 - 3x$
$8 = 5x$ Divide by 5	$\underline{-\ (-1 + 2x)}$
	$8 - 5x = 0$
	$(8 - 8) = 0$, so
	$5x = 8$

Write the simple fraction as a mixed number.

$\frac{8}{5} = x$	$x = \frac{8}{5}$
$x = 1\frac{3}{5}$	$x = 1\frac{3}{5}$

Note that the order of $2x - 1$ was changed in the subtraction.

4. You could draw the graphs in one coordinate system, but it is easier to reason mathematically and save time.

Simplify the equation $y = 8(x - 7) = 8x - 56$.

Now compare the equations.

$$y = 40 + 8x \qquad y = 8x - 56$$

Both graphs have the same slope, 8, but a different *y*-intercept so the lines are parallel. Parallel lines do *not* have an intersection point.

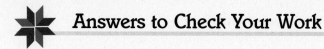

Section Ⓔ Operating with Lengths and Areas

1. All "short routes" have the same length: $4v + 6h$.

2. **a.** $(v + v + v + v) \times (h + h + h + h + h + h)$ and $4v \times 6h$ represent the area of the grid. $10vh$ does *not* represent the area, since 4 and 6 are added instead of multiplied.

   b. An expression for the area is $24vh$. Note that each small rectangle in the grid has an area of vh.

   c. You need six small rectangles. Possibilities are:
   length $6h$ and width v; $6h \times v = 6hv$ or $6vh$ (note that $vh = hv$)
   or
   length $3h$ and width $2v$; $2v \times 3h = 6vh$
   or
   length $3v$ and width $2h$; $3v \times 2h = 6vh$

3. **a.** Figure I has area $(3x)(3x) = 9x^2$.
   Figure II has area $(3x)(x) + (x)(x) + (3x)(x) =$
   $3x^2 + x^2 + 3x^2 = 7x^2$.
   Difference between area I and area II: $9x^2 - 7x^2 = 2x^2$.

   Another way you may have reasoned is:
   Observe that the cut-out sections in figure II will be the difference in the areas. The area of each of these sections is x^2, so the difference is $2x^2$.

   b. Figure II has the largest perimeter:

   $3x + x + x + x + x + x + 3x + x + x + x + x + x = 16x$

   Figure I has a perimeter of $4 \times 3x = 12x$.

4. **a.** $3(2x + 4y + 5z) + 4(x + 2y + 6z) =$ (use the distributive property)

   $6x + 12y + 15z + 4x + 8y + 24z =$ (add corresponding variables)

   $10x + 20y + 39z$

   b. $a(p + q) + a(p - q) =$

   $ap + aq + ap - aq =$

   $2ap$